PARADOX OF AWAKENING

A SPIRITUAL JOURNEY

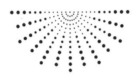

ALIZA BLOOM ROBINSON

ISBN 978-0-692-10536-8

Published by Scorpio Press

CONTENTS

PROLOGUE

The world is Awakening, I can see it, I can taste it, I witness it. We are Awakening to a deeper love, a deeper connection, a deeper caring of the planet and each other. We look out at the world and see and wonder: will we ever really wake up all the way? If the people we see are capable of more? This Awakening is beautiful, and it is messy.

Awakening can feel like a split in our awareness, in our being-ness. In this book, I share some of the lessons I've learned along the way in the form of Spiritual Paradox.

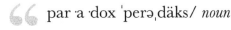 par·a·dox ˈperəˌdäks/ *noun*

a seemingly absurd or self-contradictory statement or proposition that when investigated or explained may prove to be well founded or true. *"In a paradox, he has discovered that stepping back from his job has increased the rewards he gleans from it."*

I stand for our world Awakening. I invite you to join me in taking a stand. Taking a stand is about being absolutely clear that this is our intention. Taking a stand is different than taking a position, as it is inclusive, proactive and inspires truth, authenticity and connection. I invite you to stand with me as I stand with you, as you awaken and with our planet as we awaken. In my stand I offer the following support and insights. I'd also love to hear your insights and responses. If you would like to reach out to me, there is a resource section in the back of the book with my contact information.

A world awakened is love, kindness, joy, compassion. A people awakened are people who know their Oneness with all that is and each other; who deeply care for fellow human beings. It is a world that works for all – there is enough food for all, disease is treated holistically and health, true health is the norm. The disparities of injustice, discrimination, wealth distribution and worth have evened out into sustainable enough, for everyone. Everywhere.

I wrote this book because I stand for a world Awakening. It is the very reason for my being. I stand in it and *as* it. I know that the world can be all we desire it to be. I know that love can lead the way and that in a world Awakening there is no more hate, war, hunger, or even disease. The world awakened is a world of sufficiency—where all people have all that they need in physical, material, emotional, mental and spiritual wellbeing.

INTRODUCTION

Spiritual paradox. Imperfect perfection. Destination and Journey. Oneness in Two Worlds. Alone and not alone. Bliss and the hardest work. These are paradoxical statements that occur and are experienced in the Awakening process.

WHAT IS AWAKENING?

It is a journey to yourself, not to your personality or egoic self, but through the personality and into the greater part of you, your Essence, your Higher Self, your Soul. It is a journey of becoming what you already are. A fully awakened person lives as One with the Universe, in love, kindness and compassion. A fully awakened person still lives in this world, but they are no longer of it. To *Wake Up* is to see with new eyes, in a new perspective of love for all people. Judgment dissipates, fear lessens, and love leads the way.

This world we live in is truly amazing, brilliant and beautiful.

If you are reading this, you are already on your spiritual path, you are (at least moderately) successful and life works well for you in many ways. It is also likely that you are either in a spiritual Awakening process or there is an area of your life that you are wanting a breakthrough around. It is yours for the taking. You are ready, you only need a little nudge to access an entirely new dimension of yourself and your life.

The Awakening process is not an intellectual one, it is a shifting and changing of consciousness. Your logical mind will want to run with the ideas presented. It will want to make a plan, strategize—but that will not be Awakening. It will be *thinking* about Awakening.

Awakening is a life long journey and it can happen in an instant. This book is a guide through several aspects of spiritual paradox that are experienced in the Awakening process. Each chapter explores an apparent paradox, almost opposite extremes along a spectrum. At first glance it appears that they cannot exist at the same moment, yet as we expand our consciousness and our journey of Awakening, most of us will experience both statements at the same time. The paradox is that both are true. The great perspective contains both ends and the entire spectrum at any given time.

It is the process of coming into understanding of this that leads to a deeper awareness of Awakening.

What if Awakening is simply the process of waking up from the dream or illusion of humanity? What if it is waking up from a nighttime dream, only to realize that the dream has felt more real than reality. Would it become easier to fathom?

Is the dream or illusion of humanity real or is it based in reality? What is reality, anyway? Reality is the illusion of something being real. Another paradox, really. An illusion of something being real? In metaphysics it is distinguished between relative (small r) and the Absolute. Reality is the relative experience of humanity on the planet currently.

People will say, *"Get real."* or *"Face reality."* Together, we are going to encourage you to do the opposite—to engage in the paradox—to suspend your current understanding of reality, what is real for you and take a journey to discover something new and different; expanding and opening your mind and experience to something much more real than you can imagine.

The concept of Truth, as used in this book, is the Absolute, that which is universal law, that which is greater than any person, belief or experience. The Absolute as described in these pages is my understanding and my experience of Universal principles and law. The Absolute does not change however, our understanding of Absolute can shift. Are you already beginning to see how paradox works? Our understanding includes both-and, rather than either-or. Both things are true at the same moment, even as they appear to be opposite.

For instance, most of us understand the law of gravity as that which holds us down, brings us down, keeps us firmly on the earth. Yet there is also another law, perhaps a higher one; the law of aerodynamics which allows airplanes to fly and passengers to traverse the earth at amazing speeds. Is it paradoxical to gravity? Aerodynamics does not eliminate or change gravity, but rather uses it in a different dimension of understanding. It's a bit paradoxical.

The paradoxes of spiritual law work in the same way. The law of an eye for an eye has been surpassed by Love your neighbor. The law of mind action or law of attraction is being superseded by the law of vibrational science. The laws of physicality are being transcended with the newer laws of quantum mechanics and quantum physics.

We are ever evolving spiritual beings having a spiritual adventure in human form. As we continue evolving (or Awakening), we see things with new eyes, we understand with deeper awareness and we integrate the understandings in ways that expand our consciousness. Sometimes with great ease and magical or mystical moments; other times we struggle and grapple with aspects on the journey.

Fasten your seat belts, hold on and let go! Yes, another paradox. How do you hold on and let go at the same time? Hold onto your hats and hearts and let go of attachments or expectations. The Awakening process is a ride of a lifetime and the more you surrender to the journey, the easier it becomes.

1

PERFECT AND IMPERFECT

You are perfect, whole and complete, just the way you are. Right now.

You need to change, to be different to be ok. This is the belief so many of us grew up with and perhaps still have rolling around in our heads and experiences. It traverses every aspect of our lives, from our relationships, jobs, careers, money, health, weight. This belief touches our things; our bodies, our homes, our cars as well as our beliefs about who we are and what we do.

We are spiritual beings having a human experience. Or are we human beings having a spiritual experience? Or is it that we are spiritual beings having a spiritual adventure in human experience? Does it matter?

You are perfection and the world is perfection. Yes, even when it does not appear that way. It's the spiritual paradox we are unpacking. Imperfect Perfection.

What if you knew you were perfect, that there was nothing wrong with you? Would that change your experience on the planet? What if we knew our world was perfect, even in all the imperfections we see daily? Would that change how you stand in life?

I first heard the words, "You are perfect, whole and complete" when I was in my early 20s. It struck me in a way that catapulted me into and onto my spiritual path. I'm perfect? What about this and that and I can't, and I don't... I had all the reasons that this statement could not be true for me. I leaned into it though and discovered the Truth in the words. The truth that comes only by listening deeply, by grappling through the mind and discovering both a paradox and a new way of being with myself.

This planet is messy, life experience is messy, there is no doubt. But what if life on this planet is a playground or huge studio that is only about experience? What if we are here to get messy and experience fully our humanity and in the assignment to come to life, we agree to be part of the mess and even more so part of the beauty and creation that comes from reconciling the very things that are the messiest?

What if we are here to jump into the mud pile and find ourselves? To find our sameness? To discover love and joy along with adventure? What if we are here to learn, to remember, to experience the Truth of who we are amid the mess? I believe we are and that's our mission and purpose in this lifetime.

> *Life is not a journey to the grave with the intention of arriving safely in a pretty and well-preserved body, but rather to skid in broadside, thoroughly used up, totally worn*

out, and loudly proclaiming -- WOW-- What a Ride! -
Hunter S. Thompson

I also believe that our world, and the mess we are in, is evolving and those of us who are Awakening are being called to take a stand for the greater awareness; for love and joy and peace. We are here to make a difference in the mess, not by condoning or condemning it, but by discovering our truest selves and standing in the light, bringing our brilliance to the table and from the cacophony of mess, create, discover, reveal a brand-new way of being. Sort of like creating a beautiful mosaic from a pile of broken glass.

What can come can be brilliant, radiant and include all the many pieces of humanity. As we grow and expand and realize the truth, the beauty of the whole will become apparent.

What if this life is a gift and we are free to choose what we do with it? What if it is most precious and we, meaning you, are the missing piece? What if the world needs your Awakening now? What if it's all in a divine plan for you to awaken?! This life is a gift, we are free to do with it what we please. You are the missing piece and the world needs you now. The world needs you Awakening now. The world is waiting for you, calling you, nudging you to take the next step, to cross the next barrier, to come into the next awareness of Awakening, now.

What we see in the world today is imperfection, but what if its' perfect in its apparent imperfection? We see climate change, concern for our planet. We see discrimination and inequality. We see hate and violence. We see hunger, poverty and disease, not only in third world countries, but in our own cities. We see young people crushed with the burden of life, struggling to survive. We see elderly left alone in their final hours, filled with fear and disappointment. We see "crazies" in leadership roles that can be frightening. Our media is filled with attention getting, emotional impact news, our values are questionable, and our focus of attention is on all that is wrong.

Given that we see this imperfection, can you imagine a world that works for all? Can you imagine the possibility that this imperfection is calling us to a realization of something different? Can you lean into the possibility that our focus, the addiction we have to drama, creates our reality and our experience of it?

Imagine a world Awakening, it is happening right now, concurrently with what we see on the media. Imagine a world that is beautiful, just, and in harmony. Imagine the people of this world living in love not fear; living in abundance for all rather than poverty for most; being kind, compassionate and caring for our neighbors, whether next door or across the globe.

Imagine living in a place of Oneness. It could look like this: All people know their worth and value for themselves and every other human being. We work together for a greater good in celebration and joy. Every person has access to all they need, be it food, good water, health care and friends. There would be no more boundaries or war; no more hunger or disease. We each know our Oneness and in that our thriving depends on connection with others. In that we are free to experience and express our greatest gifts and talents. There would be no more worry, struggle or strife between us and what did show up would be resolved in the healthy communication of shared values for a world that works for all.

We are in an exciting time of evolution; our world may appear to be falling apart, yet I believe it is coming to a quantum leap in consciousness. Yes, in the midst of, and even because of it being so unsettled. Life on our planet has been tempered with a sense of separation from each other and from Source for eons of time. Believing in separation has left us alone and with the impulse to fight against others and the world to survive and stay safe.

Those times are gone. As we Awaken, as we move from a mass consciousness of separation which leads to me vs them consciousness; we come into a new place. The field of Conscious Evolution, led by Barbara Marx Hubbard, calls it the Universal Human. The science of Spiral Dynamics names it the Second Tier. (Find links in the Resource Section). Mystics and shamans call it Oneness by whatever their terminology uses; Buddha consciousness, Christ Consciousness, Divine consciousness.

It is here, the time is now, and we need to each do our own work to Awaken for the planet to make this evolutionary quantum leap.

The imperfection we see is exactly perfect, because it is causing us to clean out the festering wounds that are beneath the surface of humanity. We are being called to stand up in and FOR love, compassion, kindness and basic human dignity for all people.

2

TAKING IT PERSONAL

*I*n the healing of the festering wounds of humanity comes the healing of our own personal wounds, those which we carry in our subconscious from this life-time and previous, pre-incarnation times. Wounds we carry from our lineage and the mass consciousness of the planet. Here's an obvious corollary; as we heal ourselves, the world heals and as the world heals, individuals heal. I was speaking with a woman today about this process. The healing process is evolutionary and cannot be for only one person. Each time we clear out a pattern it impacts not only those around us but seven generations forward and seven generations backwards in time.

When I answered the call, "Are you willing to serve creation?" with a YES, it was immediately followed by the statement, "then you will be asked to surrender everything." My response was, ok. What I learned over the course of the next few months was that the false beliefs, the stuck emotions, the festering wounds I was carrying in my consciousness had to be released and surrendered.

I was led through a process of freeing the emotions that I carried, both from my lifetime and as part of the mass consciousness. I discovered that the new dimension, the quantum leap into Oneness has no room for anything unlike love. So, the blame, shame, guilt that I still carried had to go. It had to be released and it wasn't a thought that did it. Everything had to go that was unlike love or neutral. It was deep healing work, a feeling of and burning up of the emotions humanity carries. It was an unraveling of all the false beliefs and stories associated with them.

We cannot take fear, anger, rage, shame, guilt or blame into the new dimension of consciousness. In the release and surrender of these deep emotions comes a healing of victim consciousness and a realization of personal responsibility for all of our life. There is no room for victim in the new consciousness, it is not recognized there. Not as if someone says, you can't enter, but the very definition of a higher plane is a higher vibration. It's a bit like separating the chaff from the wheat. As we raise our vibration into a deeper love, the chaff of victim is released, revealing only the wheat, the fruits hidden within.

We must shed our victim consciousness and all that is attached to it, to enter the narrow doorway of a higher consciousness. The density holds us down, the light brings us up. While we might be able to touch the places of bliss and awakened consciousness, we will not stay there until the vibrational patterns of less than, unworthy, anger, fear is released and transmuted. There is no space for, nor resonance to the denser emotions; for it is a consciousness of Oneness, of love. Just as there is no space for darkness in a room after the light has been turned on. It's not about judgment, right or wrong, but simply a vibrational fact.

That's not to say that we won't ever feel fear or be angry as we Awaken, but it will no longer be our dominant, go-to, or foundation of being. The emotions I mention, in and of themselves are simply energy in motion and are neither good or bad. However, the density of these emotions stuck in our consciousness, as the very fabric of our beingness on the planet are what is being called to be metamorphosed.

So we get to clean it up, clear it out. We get to do the work of surrender; a deep unraveling of emotions and beliefs like unworthiness, unlovable, not enough-ness to Love; to clear our consciousness; to be replaced with love, perfection, and Oneness.

Lean in, consider the possibility that You are perfect, perfectly imperfect perhaps, but perfect just the way you are. What if you stopped trying so hard to be different than you are. What if your work right now is to simply love who you are in your wholeness, in your fullness, in your humanity, with all your flaws and idiosyncrasies. Love and accept and allow and make friends with the places that you still want to hide. They are still there, hiding just below the surface. Let them out; let them breathe. For in breathing they can release. In hiding they maintain their form, structure and power.

Let the surrender process be gentle, like an ice cube melting in a cup of boiling water. Let it be messy, as in digging up roots of weeds in a garden. Let it be exactly what it is, as it appears, and you will be guided, supported and lifted through the process.

We cannot Awaken fully when we are still hiding dirt under the surface. We see this in the world today, you'll find someone who touts themselves as a spiritual teacher, yet you see anger or fear or inappropriate behavior lurking just below the veneer of surface. It's been uncovered with television evangelicals who are power and money hungry; with priests who abuse young children, new thought leaders who misappropriate their power over others. When we push any of our qualities away it creates resistance and keeps us from Awakening, holding us in a blind spot. When we allow and accept that the emotions or qualities are currently part of us, that they are in our field of consciousness, at least at this moment, it frees them to be shifted, subtly changed or completely transformed.

True Awakening is the journey from perfectly imperfect to perfect acceptance of who you are, at your core. It requires the deep cleaning out of the subconscious beliefs, habits, patterns and ways of being that are founded in separation.

3

ALONE AND NOT ALONE

*I*n decades past, mystics had the luxury of hiding out on the top of a hill, in a hermitage, to be the spiritual wisdom and connection for their people. Now, in our age, we are being called, not to go away from the world, but to walk in it, with greater spiritual awareness. We are One even as we live in the duality of separation.

A simple remembering at a soul level, in a mystical experience can open the door way to the journey home, home begin a return to Spirit, a return to Oneness. Yet we appear to be mired in separation. It has been determined that the greatest yearning for people, the greatest universal need we have is connection. Recently there was a study published revealing that the underlying reason for and cause of addiction is the yearning for connection or the absence of connection. See the article in Huffington Post by Johann Hari: *http://bit.ly/huffpostHari*

YOU ARE NOT ALONE

We are not alone, yet we have often felt alone. In our culture and with my work with many women there is an overwhelming, across the board, sense of isolation and separation. As women, we are coming back into an awareness of the importance of, necessity of and power of women connecting with women. As we lean into heart to heart connection with others we are seen, witnessed and connected. This does not exclude men, but rather empowers them as well.

You are not alone! You are never alone, and you can never be alone for you are One with Spirit. What about all those times you feel isolated and lonely? Why does the appearance argue with the Truth? It is our experience and our humanity; our habits and patterns.

The Awakening journey will take you into the places that have been hidden, the places we've been dissociated with and those we have judged, to clear the closet so to speak, to clear the evidence of being alone. In Truth you are never alone, you are Spirit in expression.

Lean into the words and the possibility for a moment. Suspend any evidence to the contrary and consider the possibility that right now, in this now moment, you are not alone. Can you feel your connection to the earth or the sun? Can you become aware of the air on your skin? The field of separation is strong, so strong that you may not be able to experience connection in the moment. If so, I invite you to just consider that it is possible to experience connection. Could you consider that you might not be alone in spirit.

As we begin to separate out the layers between experience and Truth, we can lean into new ways of being, listening and doing. This will lead you to discover the next pathway, the next step.

When we begin to find communities of like-minded people who are also committed to living in a state of Oneness with love, kindness and compassion, our journey can quicken. Every time we join in unity, our Presence expands, and our impact enlarges.

It is time for collaboration, for sisterhood, for communities to stand with and for each other and the planet. We see this in the many grassroots movements popping up, with seemingly little effort. An example would be the Women's March day following our last presidential inauguration, in which it is estimated over 4 million people participated with organized activities in over 650 cities, with seemingly little effort. It began with a small group of people, entered the social media world and exploded. This is evidence of shared values, coming together for a greater good.

As we continue along our Awakening journey it is beneficial to find a like-minded community, to connect with others along the journey and to stay engaged with the world. As much as we'd love to disengage, it is imperative to bring our Awakening to the world, for this is where the work lies. Yes, a spiritual paradox. We are being called to bring our light and love to the world in ways that haven't been as necessary as they are now.

YOU, ALONE...

It does not happen overnight in most cases, but it can happen with diligence and vigilance in spiritual practice. It is a process of surrender. Surrendering all egoic attachments, to titles, status, things, beliefs, emotions and everything that is neither neutral or unlike love. It's like the peeling of an onion; it's like the caterpillar going to mush before being reformed into a butterfly. It's beautiful, it can be painful, exquisitely profound and unlike anything you've ever experience before.

The Awakening process is getting easier, however. In recent decades, we have been given technology and science as well as awareness to transcend our humanity quicker and easier than in the past. This technology is not the computer-type, but a spiritual technology that provides teachings, access points and pathways. It has evolved in ways that Oneness and Awakening are now accessible to anyone who desires it.

The amount of pain and suffering we go through in the process is related, at least in part, to our resistance and to our holding on. Things like being right, comparison, judgment are the things that hold us back. Love, grace, forgiveness opens the pathways.

It's like the ones who have gone before us have macheted a path through the jungle. With each passing the path is easier to find, becomes easier to navigate and is creating new neuropathways in consciousness that we all can benefit from. It also depends on what you hold in your consciousness, primarily your un- and sub-consciousness. Those can be the hardest patterns to discover and break. In these instances, even as it is beneficial to have a trusted advisor or guide helping to shine the light of consciousness in places we cannot see ourselves, the work of surrender must be done by you. You alone can surrender.

We can drop the illusion or separation anytime we truly desire to do so. Yes, unfortunately, it has been engrained into our subconscious for near eternity, but we now have the technology, through the application of quantum science to rewrite the subconscious beliefs. We need only to identify them and their origination to re-write the story and thereby change our entire lives.

First, however, we must come to believe in the Truth that there is no separation. It is only an illusion. We are, you are enough, you are love, you are One with all that is. You are One with the very God that created you in the beginning of time, One with all of humanity and One with the universe itself.

There can be no more judgment when you realize Oneness. It's a lot to give up. Are you willing to give up the stories you believe? Are you willing to surrender the beliefs you hold so dear? Are you willing to let go of your superiority to discover your Truth? It's a lot to give up. And, you must be willing to do so to realize Oneness.

The pathway through is discovered by opening your heart. When immersed in the experience of separation this appears to be the craziest and most impossible thing to do; yet clearing the barriers around your heart and allowing the love to flow will open the doorways to Oneness.

The Awakening process is an Awakening and freeing of the deeper spiritual heart. Most of us have our hearts so buried beneath protective barriers, obstacles and layers of blockages, that freeing the heart takes time. It happens in and through the Awakening process. Freeing the heart causes spiritual Awakening. And spiritual Awakening frees the heart.

The more love and Oneness we experience and express the more the heart opens. The more the heart opens the more love and Oneness can be expressed. In opening our hearts, we begin to release more ways of being that no longer serve us.

PRACTICE

Here are two simple practices to support your journey.

Practice self-love. Self-loathing is prevalent on the planet. It must go. Begin to love yourself unconditionally, through and through, all the parts of you; the good, the bad; the brilliant and the ugly. As you love these aspects of yourself, you will be able to love them in another. Until you do, you will live in judgment of others which will keep you from Oneness.

Pay attention to what you think. Where can you be kinder, where can you be more loving, to yourself and then to others? Open your heart to Love. Open your heart to Truth. Opening your heart will begin to dissolve the obstacles. Dismantling barriers to love will open your heart. It is a spiral and mutually dependent process. Notice how you judge yourself and others, then reframe it. Notice how you talk to yourself and others, then be kinder. Be gentle with yourself. There are eons of patterns to unravel and it can happen.

It is imperative to find support on your journey, for as you are discovering, you are not alone, you cannot do the deeper work alone and you must do it alone. Yes, another paradox. As you dive into the deeper layers of clearing out the subconscious, of clearing the sludge or dross of humanity that we each carry in our unconscious it is crucial to have assistance.

You cannot do it alone and you must do it alone.

The ego is basically the conscious mind, the part of your identity that you consider your "self", fueled by the subconscious mind. While the ego has its good points, and benefits us in many ways it also can be a bit like Jekyll and Hyde. On and off, up and down, supportive and sabotaging. To keep this discussion simple and on focus, we simply say that the ego, when subservient to the heart or soul becomes an ally. But left in charge it can wreak havoc.

The Awakening process is a shift from ego-based consciousness to heart-based consciousness. And to make this shift, you need a facilitator to guide you beyond your ego; shine the light of consciousness into the hidden. Then work of dismantling and processing through surrender of the emotions carried there must be done alone. For no one can do that for you, but you.

There are several reasons for this. The first is that it is impossible to see what you cannot see. Until you see it, that is. The Awakening process involves dismantling our blind spots. If we could see them, they would not be blind. Becoming aware is the first step.

You can't do it alone because the Awakening process dismantles the egoic and personality aspects of being, transferring them from front end leadership to their rightful place of subservience to the heart. Of course, the ego and the personality will fight this tooth and nail.

You must do it alone. Once you see it, the work of surrender and transcending is up to you, no one can do the inner work for you.

My experience is the ego can be a sneaky, subtle energy that derails my Awakening process. It has been created through life experiences and is mostly unconscious. The ego has a very important role in our life, but we've given it way too much power. The ego is the culmination of the subconscious and personality, which includes all the wounds and false beliefs we hold unaware. We have many aspects to our beingness and ego is the word I'm using here to gather all the pieces.

In the spiritual world, the ego often gets a bad rap. There have been movements to completely dismantle it and destroy it; getting rid of it entirely. This is not necessary, but what is necessary it to put it in its correct role. An analogy would be that the unhealed, untethered ego is a child and the integrated higher heart wisdom is an adult. When a person is stressed the child comes to the surface and tries to run the show or drive the car. When we can identify that we are operating from a sense of what we could call wounded self, we can stop, readjust and choose again. In driving the car, we instruct the ego to get in the back seat, and allow the adult to drive the car. In simplest terms the ego operates from fear much of the time and the heart operates in love always.

Another loose analogy is that the experience of the ego is contraction and the heart is expansion.

The correct role of the ego is to be subservient to the higher heart. When the ego is in its rightful place, life works smoother. We will be no longer run by fear or protection, but allowing Love to lead the way from that place of Being in your Heart.

4

GET YOUR OWN DIRT

*W*hile it might be our experience, and although we can cite facts and evidence to support it, the belief that we are alone and separate is simply not true. We are not separate. We have never been separate. We could never be separate from Creation, from the initial sparkle of unique brilliance that we were created to be.

One of my favorite stories is of a scientist challenging God. "God was once approached by a scientist who said, "Listen God, we've decided we don't need you anymore. These days we can clone people, transplant organs and do all sorts of things that used to be considered miraculous."

God replied, "Don't need me huh? How about we put your theory to the test. Why don't we have a competition to see who can make a human being, say, a male human being."

The scientist agrees, so God declares they should do it like he did it the good old days when he created Adam.

"Fine" says the scientist as he bends down to scoop up a handful of dirt."

"Whoa!" says God, shaking his head in disapproval. "Not so fast. You get your own dirt."

Get your own dirt. I love that phrase because it brings me back to Oneness, to the awareness that I cannot be separate from the whole. We, too, in physical form are created from the same dirt, and air, and particles. We are now and never could be otherwise.

In the beginning when the individualized sparkles of light began to grow and expand in consciousness there was only Oneness. We were all One. There was only divine love, light and joy. In the sacred space of Oneness there was peace.

The impulse for experience and expansion continued, and our belief in separation grew. As a result, we find ourselves in the place we are today, in our world, on our planet. In the world of today we see fear, anger, hatred, injustice, inequality, and violence. We see all the evidence that we are not safe, not connected, and certainly not One with all others. We think we are alone. Loneliness is a growing health epidemic, and is said to be as potentially destructive as smoking, obesity and other pathologies. Former Surgeon General, Vivek H. Murthy reports that over 40% of adults in America report feeling lonely.

That's staggering and many people I know have had experiences of being intensely lonely. So how can we say we are not alone? It's a spiritual paradox. One that we can take concrete action to shift. Recently I was working with a circle of 10 women; each one of them expressed a challenge of being or feeling isolation. These women were spiritual Awakening, successful, healthy and engaged people. Yet, the sense of isolation was prevalent. I echoed the experience.

In our digital age, with our virtual connections, it is easy to slide away from real and meaningful connections. I spend many hours each week in the virtual world, working with clients and groups through a computer screen and video technology. While it is wonderful, we still crave the human touch, being in the same room, hugs and clinking our cups together in shared space.

In truth, the connection we seek is not only with others, but also with Spirit, that which is greater than us. We are not separate, we are not alone. The shift is to consciously connect to others in meaningful ways, to step outside of our comfort bubble and reach out. Or in. Inward, meaning touching the stillness within, touching the space within that is filled with love, light and connection.

We think we are merely humans, some with super powers, but it is not true. We are not merely human in the same way we are not the clothes we wear, the hair style we have or the car we drive. The connection we seek is not only for someone outside of us to love us, to affirm us, to tell us we are ok, it is a deeper seeking. One that gets satiated only by shifting out of our minds and the mental loops we live in and entering our hearts and souls. We are much, much more. We are Spirit embodied, Creation personified. We are that which is the very Source emanating as Us, individual expressions of the light.

Although it might be our experience and we have facts to support it, it is simply not true. We are not separate, never have been separate and could never be separate from Creation, from the initial sparkle of unique brilliance that we were created to be.

The work of Awakening is to realize, remember and reconnect to the aspect of our Selves that has always known our connection, to the Truth of who we are and who we are becoming. Our Soul, our Spirit, our Essence, which is ever present and ever connected in Oneness is never alone.

To release the grips of separation, we must transcend our ego and personality. This we cannot do by ourselves. Oh, it might have happened for a mystic or two, but likely not for most of us. For the rest of us, it takes a traumatic or revolutionary experience that shocks our systems into deep change, or it requires another outside of us, to shine the light into the darkness, to uncover the deeply hidden egoic aspects. Without this, we awaken within the context of ego, and this is not true Awakening at all.

The true work of Awakening is to transcend the ego, not in getting rid of it, or squashing it, but in the process of the ego becoming subservient to the heart or the Spirit, this is the work. It is a dismantling and a transcending of the egoic self that leads to release of judgment and comparison.

5

DESTINATION OR JOURNEY?

Just do it! - Nike

*I*s it possible to Awaken in an instant and have it be complete? It might be; there are some mystics who have had this as their experience. However, for most of us, it is both a destination and a journey.

The journey of Awakening is a daily process, no matter how awake you are, there is another layer of expansion and expression of that Oneness. The destination of Awakening is Oneness.

We are ever evolving, ever expanding as individuals, as souls and as creation, so even as Oneness is touched, there is another expansion happening. In any given moment you can experience Oneness. Likely you have, many times. The awakened moment can happen any time you are fully present to what is. The birth of a baby; a mystical experience in meditation or elsewhere; the awe and wonder of a sunset or sunrise; the laughter of a child; your own belly laughter, making love or deep conversations with friends.

An awakened moment transcends time and space, it is beyond the mind. In fact, as soon as you notice the expanded state you are in, it shifts. This is because in the noticing, the mind clicks in and in the expanded space, there is no mind active.

From the beginning of time creation has been expanding. Science tells us that we are either expanding or contracting; growing or dying. Science also has proven that there is no end to the Universe. We used to believe the Earth was flat; that the Earth was the only planetary system; we were the one and only universe, but that is no longer our belief system. We have evolved to seeing and believing more than ever before. Now, scientists have proven multiple universes.

I've experienced it, I've been taken to places that far exceed my mind. As you read this next paragraph of my experience, lean into it and feel the experience for yourself.

I was in a meditation, having gone down, down, down into my being. From my physical body into my heart space. Getting smaller and smaller, going deeper and deeper, I came to a still point, a portal. As I entered that portal, I entered the cosmos. I was taken on a journey through space from our solar system, into a black hole that showed me infinite other systems, on and on and on until I came to the end of what I could see. It was black space, pure potentiality, creation undefined. It was expansive and brilliant, even in the darkness. I realized in my being, the ever evolving, ever expanding, never ending field of the infinite.

This experience was more than a meditation, for it changed me at depth. In my personalized introduction to the cosmos, my mind was blown wide open. As a result, I began to see life differently; I began to see a greater picture and realized in my beingness the spiral of evolution and the infinity of creation.

In the beginning before we were, there was a nothingness, a no-thing-ness, and there came an impulse so great that Creation happened. First there was light, then land and water, then life, In the beginning before there was humanity, there was an impulse of Beingness. This Beingness was so great, it was light and love. It filled the interspaces of the Universe. There was an impulse so great within this Beingness that humanity was created, first as individualized sparkles of light. Imagine the rainbow colors of light through a crystal, or the sparking dew on a spring morning.

As human beings, we were given free will that caused us to want to do it alone. The short and simple version is that we created the illusion of separation, so we could prove to ourselves that we did not need Spirit, that we were smart enough, good enough to create our lives alone.

There then began a dream; the Toltecs, Sufis and Eastern traditions call it Maya. Maya is defined as the power by which the universe becomes manifest; the illusion or appearance of the phenomenal world. To have experience and be on this planet, we stepped into this dream of illusion. The great dark came upon the world when the unique particle began to think they were separate based in the uniqueness. Within the manifestation of the world as we know it, Maya or the illusion, of our experience is of separation.

As we took human form and adjusted to the dream we forgot that separation was the illusion, we began to believe it and in that belief lost our sense of connection. In truth we are One with all that is but collectively, we have chosen to believe in something else. (There is a chapter in my book, *Falling Into Ease*

– *Release Your Struggle and Create A Life You Love*, [*http://amzn.to/2CmjrLC*] about seeing and believing. In that we can only see what we believe, and we can't see what we do not believe.)

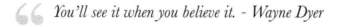 *You'll see it when you believe it. - Wayne Dyer*

Over time we forgot the illusion of separation was illusion and we over and falsely empowered our egos and chaos ensued. Before long, we so believed in separation that everything evolved around self-preservation and competition and comparison and judgement and fighting began. We began feeling less than, not enough, unworthy and here we find ourselves millennia later alone, struggling, fighting and so afraid.

Maya came up on the humanity as a race and the idea of separate became engrained in each person. Some, however are beginning to awaken from that dream. We are all One. There is nothing that is separate from the one. The little finger and the big toe are individuated (individualized) body parts, but all One body. The liver and the heart and the spleen are individual, unique organs, but all of One Body. Each person on the planet is individual and yet part of the One, the Oneness. When One hurts, the whole is affected. When One heals, the whole heals. There is tradition, especially with the Navajo's, that when we heal emotional wounds, we are healing our ancestral lineage up to seven generations back and seven generations forward. We are also healing the cosmic and collective consciousness.

The destination is Oneness, the full embodiment of our Essence, expressing as and in Oneness, with all our unique gifts, purpose, passions and connection to the world. We can have moments of reaching the destination, but those are moments, the true Awakening is living in and from that state of consciousness. The repetition and frequency of an awakened moment can build new pathways, and lead to the awakened state. This is our goal, if we can say that. It is our intention, desire and where we are headed.

The journey is the process of becoming that which we already have within us, that which we are becoming. It's evolution, it's growth, its expansion at its best and at its core. The journey is the process of letting go, being filled, surrender, acceptance and the integration and embodiment of the new truth, the new awareness which leads to different perspectives and perceptions.

The journey can be likened to a hike up a mountain. With each new bend a new vista is visible. The destination is of course the intention, but the enjoyment, each moment of the journey is important, effective and filled with possibilities of new.

I was on a hike one time, it was quite steep, and we were deep in the woods. The path was narrow and rocky, so my attention was on where I put my feet. The sun was dappling through the leaves of the trees. There is a Japanese word that describes it beautifully: komorebi: if you've ever wandered through a thicket, jungle, or forest before, you've experienced this: the closest translation is sunlight that filters through the leaves of trees and onto the forest floor. It has my attention and nothing else.

My friend was ahead of me. She called out to me, "Oh wow, look at this beautiful lake and the views from here." From where I was there was no lake, no views other than trees and splotchy light. With her encouragement, I continued and only a few yards up the path, the trees opened and there was the most beautiful majestic mountain lake and stunning vistas. We could see all the way across it and up onto the next mountain. The sun was shining, gleaming, sparkling on the smooth waters.

If this moment in the journey had been our destination, we would have been fulfilled. Yet there was more, we had not yet reached the destination we were heading towards. We took time to enjoy the unexpected blessing, to bask in the beauty and to rest along the way. Then we were off again, on the journey.

When we enjoy each plateau, each moment, along our journey, life becomes richer, sweeter and more sacred. Do not rush past the blessings and do not stop there either. Open yourself to blessings both expected and unexpected. Open yourself to see with new eyes, the eyes of a greater perspective, a higher vision. For each step along the way there is possibility for new and uncharted territory, experience and perspectives.

6

AWAKE OR ASLEEP?

> *Awake, asleep, awake, asleep, sort of awake, daydreaming,*
> *sleeping restlessly, dreaming deep, awake again or asleep?*
> *How awake are you? Or "Are You Sleepwalking Through*
> *your Awakening?"*

- Rev. Dr. Jane Simmons [*http://amzn.to/2EOJcFT*]

To be fully awakened is like being pregnant, you either are or you are not. But the Awakening process, the journey of Awakening is filled with subtleties and nuances of being awake and asleep. The good news is that the more you awaken the less you drift back into a hard sleep. There will be moments of dozing, or dreaming or even taking a good hard sleep in the journey, but you will never be as asleep as you were yesterday. You can't go backwards, even as you continue along the journey. It is a spiral, so when it feels like you are back at the same spot you were before, do not worry, you are coming around to a similar place, but in a new state of consciousness. It's a paradox and it's a process.

By keeping your eyes open, both literally and spiritually, you will stay awake. To slip back into slumber is to close your eyes to the beauty, the blessings that are all around us, no matter what the situation or circumstance you find yourself in.

If you are climbing a tough climb, be ready for an unexpected vista, a new view or a surprise lake to bask in. If you notice you are falling asleep, call yourself on it and do something that causes you to raise your vibration. For example, use a simple practice of distraction to remind yourself to find beauty, joy, love, kindness and compassion. Distract yourself from your slumber by focusing on your breath, by basking in beauty, or by consciously moving into appreciation.

We will all have moments of crystal-clear clarity, it will feel like we are wide awake, that the screen of our lives just shifted from an old tube color television to one with high definition. My husband had cataract surgery a few years ago. Following the surgery, he kept saying that it was like the HD television – everything looked different, the colors were brighter, the sky was brilliant. He couldn't get over the difference he was experiencing.

Staying awake is remembering to see the bright colors of the world. It is staying in gratitude and appreciation. It is staying awake to the journey you are on and to the destination right in front of you. It can be easy after an Awakening moment, a mystical moment, to slowly shift back into what used to be normal. Resist the temptation to shrink, to settle back into normalcy. Instead stretch into a new normal, allow the new to integrate through your being and hold your vision at the highest degree possible.

If you notice the colors of your life are getting subtler, or dimmer, do something different. Go outside, look up. See differently. Be with young children. Laugh. Take a break, or even a nap, then wake up again. Take time to reconnect to the memory of the brilliance and become the vibration of that memory once again.

BEING PRACTICE

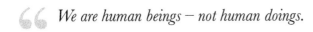 *We are human beings — not human doings.*

When we figure this out we will have discovered a very important key. Focus not on what you should do, but on how you want to Be.

A client of mine said recently, "It's so easy to really Be the Love when we are together, in retreat or in the conscious of a sacred container. What I want is to Be Love, all the time, out in the world." This takes conscious awareness, diligence and vigilance on what we are putting our attention on and where we allow ourselves to be pulled back into slumber.

What are the qualities of being that you want to embody today? Some examples might be loving, kind, creative, expansive, compassionate, abundant, generous.

What would you choose to Be today? Then find at least three ways, outside of the normalcy of your daily life to implement and Be them. Take your new Being into the world and play with it. If you were Being this how would life show up differently?

If you were to stay awake, who would you BE? Who would

you want to Be? If you desire it, it lives within you, it's already there. Take it on like a mantle, like a role and see how it fits. This deep desire comes from the depths of your being, so do not worry if it feels fake, it's the real you looking for escape from the normalcy of who you are acting as.

Being this new refreshed, recalibrated you, what do you notice? At the end of the day, take a few moments to write your experience. What did you notice? How did it feel? From this place of Being, what did you do that might have been different from before?

7

UNIQUE IN OUR ONENESS

 ith our ego in its proper place and our heart leading the way in Love, we access a different aspect of our souls and begin to come into alignment with our innate gifts, talents and soul purpose on the planet. We are not alone; we cannot awaken fully by ourselves and we have to do it (the inner healing) alone. It's a mouthful, a handful and a mind boggler, its paradoxical.

> *We are the ones we've been waiting for.*
>
> - *June Jordan*

Now is the time to fulfill your purpose on this planet. Now is the time that we have been waiting for and we are the Ones. It is time to let go everything that is unlike love. Surrender your identification and your attachment to all that is outside of you. Our great grand purpose is to Awaken, to come into realization of our Oneness. Within that purpose, however, we each have individual gifts, talents, dreams and visions that will come into being with our Awakening.

One way into the awakened state is to raise and attune to the vibrations of Truth. We are vibrational beings and our vibration is indicative of how we are feeling. In the work of Abraham there is an emotional guidance scale; in David Hawkins' work he uses a consciousness scale. Both tools speak into the vibration of emotions and states of being. In the raising of vibration, there is more energy present and we feel better. There is no judgment for the vibrations lower on the scale and the intention is to grow into a higher vibration.

It's a little like moving through the evolution of schooling, starting with preschool and kindergarten, moving up the scale through elementary, middle and high schools then perhaps going on into higher education. Everyone goes through the stages and it is difficult to bypass them.

As we move through the vibrational scale into love, everything that is unlike love must go. In my early days of spiritual initiation there was a phrase that guided our surrender process. "Surrender anything and everything that is neither neutral or love." That means fear, anger, judgment. That means unworthiness, comparison and separation. It sounds beautiful, doesn't it?

It is the processing through the lower vibrations that opens the pathways to higher ones. Although we can touch the higher ones, we cannot stay there until we have healed the wounding or stuck-ness of the lower frequencies.

For me, it was a process of working through the subconscious and healing, transcending the denser spots. It was exquisite and excruciating. Some emotions were released, dissolved or dismantled with ease, others not so much. Others including shame, anger and rage had to burn through my being to be fully released. This process freed my soul to not only touch the higher vibrational states, but to live there. It sounds almost too good to be true. But it is true. The time is now. We are the Ones we've been waiting for – no longer outside of us, but Us, personally and collectively.

It's time to wake up. The awakened state is something to be achieved, to strive for, but not exactly. Yes, there is a reaching, but not a mental striving or even physical one. This is spiritual work. It is the work of surrender, forgiveness and clearing to make room for pure love. It is the work for which we are on the planet. The vibration of Oneness is already available and accessible to all.

The pathways are being cleared, the way is being made open. It is time to land in the vibration of love and to live in and through and from that consciousness of Oneness.

Here's the cincher - you must release within yourself, surrender or dismantle all that is unlike love. That includes fear, anger, resentment and more. And for those emotions and patterns to be transcended you must feel them, accept them, acknowledge them first. It is our resistance to what is that causes our suffering. As Paul Selig says in his work, *I Am the Word*, [*http://amzn.to/2Crvw57*] "It's not an easy path, and it's only not easy because it moves things." He goes on in the next paragraph, "It doesn't need to be hard at all, and all that is hard is your attachment to the regulations you have placed on the self for the self to be and see and experience the world in a certain way. That's all there is to it." It doesn't have to be hard, it is your resistance that makes it hard. But it does have to be felt.

So, if you are feeling something, feel it through to the end. If you touch anger, feel it until it flows through you. If you are feeling fear, turn around and look it in the face, lean into it until it begins to dissipate. If you are feeling depressed, dive into it until you come through it.

So many of us resist what we call the darker emotions, the ones that don't feel good. Emotions are energy in motion. They only become problematic when they get stuck, or denied, or buried into the subconscious.

It is time to release them. It is time to allow yourself to be drawn into the higher vibration of the Christ consciousness. The good news and the bad news is - you can't take the heavy emotions with you. We are not in judgment of denser emotions, but they are not possible in the higher realms.

You are enough, you are love, you are loved, and you are loveable forever. You are good enough and better than that. You are worthy. There is nothing you must do to receive or achieve Spirit's love. It is there for you unconditionally and forever. You need do nothing. The true impulse within you to serve and to give to humanity, to make a difference in the world is pure. At times, it can get tainted with the unworthiness issues so many of us are still dealing with.

You need nothing. And you are called into action, for what better way to experience life on this amazing planet than to engage with it. Another paradox – do nothing; take action. Clear out the messy strings of unworthiness and not enough-ness. Find the purest intention that is soul directed and do that. A soul directed action is one that comes inspired, from the depths of silence rather than from the busyness of your mind. Action when taken from the stillness of being has very different intentions and results than action taken from a sense of being busy to be busy.

SOUL DIRECTED ACTION PRACTICE

I often get the question; how do I know if my action is soul directed or ego directed? Here is an uncomplicated way to practice listening to the difference.

First get still. Quiet your body, mind and spirit. Plant your feet onto the ground and take a few deep slow breaths. Notice where your attention is. Begin to consciously move it around. Feel your head, face, hands, feet, belly, torso and heart. Notice how each area may feel a bit differently. Bring your awareness to your thinking head, to the place of your thoughts and notice how your body responds.

Bring your awareness to your deeper spiritual heart, that place behind your physical heart, in the center of your being. Notice how your body responds here.

Without looking for the answer quite yet, ask yourself the question, "what is mine to do....?" Ask it first from your thinking head. Notice your body sensations. Notice the thoughts processing, looking for the right answer.

Shifting your awareness to your deeper spiritual heart and ask the question there, "what is mine to do..."? Again, without looking for the answer, notice how your body responds differently. Now, gently open to receive the answer from your deeper spiritual heart.

Typically, the answers that are soul-directed will be gentler, quieter, simpler. They will come with a sense of ease and expansion. The thinking head responses will be more complicated and come with a greater sense of urgency, a busyness or several steps all at once.

When you notice that there are too many things floating around, drop back into your body and your deeper spiritual heart. Listen quietly for the next best step.

(What is Mine to Do...? A Guided Process for Spiritual Discernment is available on Amazon http://amzn.to/2CAV2pB and in audio format.)

8

TAKE A BREAK

*I*t is important even in our Awakening to give it a rest. Awakening is not supposed to be arduous work. Yes, you must be diligent and vigilant in your process. Yes, it goes much smoother if you have a dedicated and committed practice. At some point, the practice becomes beingness. At some point the practices become simply the ways you operate in your life.

So many of us go at breakneck speeds through our lives, forgetting that life is a gift; an experience to be enjoyed, cherished and luxuriated in. Imagine going to a fine dinner out in a nice restaurant. Do you not settle in and enjoy each course as it arrives and indeed the time between the courses as well? Of course, you do. Begin living life in this manner as well.

The time that you are sitting, simply sit. The times that you are drinking your tea or coffee, simply enjoy those time. The times that you are writing or preparing a course, simply be present to that activity. If you are cooking or cleaning, or playing, simply relax into the activity.

So many of us live in an experience of having too much to do and not enough time to do it. In talking with a friend and colleague recently, she mentioned that she just simply could not get her to do list tackled. There was too much on it. I agreed with her and told her that I shared her experience. In that week, my list to do was growing each day not shrinking, so I completely understood. And yet, when we let go, drop our resistance and relax just even a bit, life flows so much easier.

How can we relax when we are all tied up in knots? Begin to make it conscious practice. Some simple practices I give my clients are reminders to come into the present moment. Feel your feet on the ground. Notice your breath, follow it and allow it to become deeper. Look up. Walk away. Drop your shoulders.

When life gets tough, keep going. When life slows down, quit pushing. So, which is it? Keep pushing or quit pushing? My simple answer is this, if you are in a denser energy vibration and emotions, such as overwhelm, fear or stress are showing up, quit pushing. It appears to be counter intuitive, but from a denser energy the push is only creating resistance. Instead, quit pushing, take a break, go outside and find a way to raise your vibration.

The inner work that is taking place is equally important to the outer work. If you notice you are pushing or trying too hard it is time to go within and care for your Self. When you are renewed, refreshed or in a higher vibration, embody it fully then return to the tasks at hand. Take time to integrate all the shifts and changes you've been through, drawing the fullness of them into your being, letting them settle and then the next outer step will be easier. If you try too soon to return to the outer world, things may seemingly backfire, only because you are not quite integrated yet.

If on the other hand, your vibration is high, and you are living in the flow, this is the time to push. Push in and from the higher vibration of love, creativity, purpose and passion. From and in the higher vibration, go the extra mile, use the momentum to continue your projects.

We have it all backwards, we tend to push when things aren't going well, but that creates useless and unnecessary suffering. We don't even know how much we push. We don't even realize how it would be to surrender fully to the process. What if you were to take a few moments each time you notice you are pushing and back off. Back away, turn around and see if there is another way, an easier way. What can you do with yourself to come into a greater flow?

Keep your eye and your vibration on what you'd love. How do you want to feel? Do you want to feel happy? Then be happy, find ways to activate the feeling of happy. Do you want joy? Find ways to bring joy into your life. Do you want to feel accomplished, then activate the feeling of accomplished even before you do anything? Do you want to feel peace? Activate peace within yourself first. Do it without pushing or forcing.

RELAX PRACTICE

Can you relax just a bit more? Can you let go and simply enjoy the process? All is well, everything is in movement. You cannot control the outcome, so why try so hard? You are already in Spirit's graces, you are adored, and supported fully, so relax. You have nothing to prove. You being you is enough. You are bringing your light into the world, no matter what you are doing, it is enough. Even with your desires and goals and intentions, find a spacious, relaxed vibration first. Ask yourself the deeper question. What is behind the desire for striving? Are you still trying to prove yourself? Or is it something different?

As you become aware of what is underneath your desires, begin to shift to an awareness of how it would feel when you have it. What would you love and how might that play out in your life? Lean into a vibration of being relaxed, trusting with all your heart that it is already so.

9

NOTHING WRONG

*W*e have a lifetime of untangling to do; untangle it; unravel it one step at a time. Surrender is the key, we try too hard to get it right. Let it be. Value what you value without judgment. Desire what you desire without judgement. This planet is about experience and ultimately about love. Love is the essence of Being.

Love yourself, love your life, love right where you are and who you are. From that place of deep and abiding love, you will be guided to take the next action; to speak the next words; to do what you are here on the planet to do. Love, express, create. That is all. Service becomes part of it, but not from the idea of needing to serve, more from a place of natural expression, as an outcome to the inner work.

Keep untangling, keep unraveling, you are close. Keep your eye on Love, keep your attention on love. Love. Love. That is all there is. There is great support from the invisible realms in our Awakening. When we desire, when we ask, the support is real. Each time you become aware of that, the denser energies are freed so that you can access more and more of the real you.

Consider this, what if, right now, there is nothing wrong. You don't have to do anything at all, except read on and see what comes into your awareness.

In Truth, in the Absolute, you cannot be broken. You are the light of the world. As you awaken you discover a switch you can flip. There is a story about a young man who was immersed in the world of gangs and drugs, as he was getting clean and taking his life back again, he dreamed about coming into a pitch-black warehouse. It was so dark, he couldn't see anything. Then he came to a light switch by feeling his way along a wall and discovered a switch. As he flipped the switch the warehouse was filled with light and lots of it! In his dream, he said, "I never even knew it was there." He had no idea that light was accessible and available to him. Then he wept in telling his dream to his mentor, for his brother who had just died, never had the opportunity to flip the switch.

Flip your switch. You are the light of the world and you belong in the world for this time. Let your light so shine. Infuse everything you do with your light, the light of above, of greater than you. It is easy to hide beneath a shroud, but remove it now. This is the time for light. This is time to stretch beyond your comfort zones and expand and play with the players who are all around you. They are here, they might be hiding, just like you, but they are here.

When you wonder if you are in the right place. Look down. Where are your feet? If they are below you, you are in the right place. Does it look perfect? Does it matter? You are here for a reason, a season. Your light is important in this moment right where you are. If you don't like the place you find yourself, flip the switch. Raise your vibration. Look up, see beauty. Look for good and you will find it, it is there.

Take time today to activate your light and let it shine. Shine it in your community, shine it in your home. Shine it in your Being. Let it out. I promise you, you will like it! Even in the midst of not knowing, during whatever challenge you might be facing, open and allow. Open and shine let the light that is within out into the world.

FLIP YOUR SWITCH MEDITATION

Take a moment to experience the sense of flipping your switch in three different scenarios.

Like the young man in the story above, imagine yourself standing in a warehouse that is completely pitch black. Feel into the darkness, lean into the inability to see. Feel the heaviness. Reach out and flip a switch and see the warehouse illuminated fully. Look around at all you can see and sense with the light on in the warehouse. Perhaps the answer to your question is right there, or the pathway is made clear.

Imagine now sitting very comfortably in a dark forest. You know you are safe. The sun has gone down, and it is now the deep silky, black of a moonless night. Become aware of a glimmer of light deep within your own being. A dimmer knob appears in your hand like magic. Slowly turn the switch and see the glimmer of light within you become a candle flame. Continue turning the light up as it becomes a lantern. You have the light within yourself and the ability to turn it on, anytime.

Imagine the lantern of light that is within you, now becomes you. You are the lantern of light; the light is emanating from every cell of your being. Turn the switch on and you light up the world. You are the light of the world. You are the light you've been seeking, and you can turn on your light at any moment. When you are complete, come into gratitude. And so it is.

NOTICE WHAT YOU NOTICE

*a*s we begin to notice what we notice, we can discover when we are feeling less than at ease; with that aware-ness we can make conscious choice about how we are feeling and what we are focusing on. From there we can choose to go with the feeling or to interrupt the pattern and make a new choice. The body is a wonderful tool for identifying how we are vibrating. When we are feeling good, we are in an expan-sive state and vibrating highly.

On the other hand, if we are feeling badly, whether that be physically, emotionally or mentally, it is an indicator that we are vibrating at a lower level, that there is either a thought or emotion that is causing contraction.

By becoming consciously aware we can interrupt the pattern. First notice it, then choose again. If you are having a tough time making a shift, then do something different. Go outside, look up, dance or move your body. Listen to great music or walk away from what you are doing.

Make it a practice to notice how you are feeling. Catch the downward spiral of contraction as soon as you can, and you'll begin to experience significant shifts in your overall being.

NOTICING PRACTICE

Here's a practice –

Notice what you notice about how you are feeling. Name the emotion underlying all the thoughts you are having about it. Simply notice, don't try to change them. Where do you feel this in your body? Can you place it? Does it have a shape or color to it? Acknowledge them and accept that this is your current emotional state.

Bring your awareness down to your feet connected to the earth and really feel your vibration, what does it feel like, in the emotional state? Now drop it, shift your awareness up through your body, feet, hips and into your heart. From your heart look up to the Absolute, call in the vibration of Love, Choose it instead. Allow your entire energy field to align with Love (or gratitude or appreciation).

Take a few moments to allow the shift. Notice what you notice. Does your body change? Your thoughts? Feel the new vibration and frequency. What does that feel like in your being? Can you place it in your body? Does it have a color or shape or essence? Any moment you choose to remember, you can do this practice and shift your vibration.

This is the surrender process. Surrendering, giving up, ceasing to resist the bad feelings and giving your authority over to Love. It's quite simple and a lovely experience. The practice and work is to remember to do it.

The surrender process clears a dense energy to create space within our being for a lighter vibration. According to the laws of the Universe, an empty space cannot remain empty, so when there is space it will be filled again. We can fill the open space with love and light or the antidote to what was released. For example, as you surrender and release anger, consciously fill it with compassion. Let the vibration of compassion penetrate and fill the open spaces of your being.

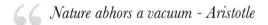 *Nature abhors a vacuum - Aristotle*

Everyone has an upper limit, that place of acceptance of our good whether it is health, love, abundance or joy. This is the level of receiving that has been programmed into our subconsciousness. Without conscious stretching of our upper limit, it will return to balance every time. Gay Hendricks wrote a wonderful book, *The Big Leap*, [*http://amzn.to/2CxoFIi*] thoroughly exploring the concepts of how we sabotage our success with upper level limit problems. We get a windfall of cash then get sick. We fall in love and then have a crisis that keeps us unavailable. Maria Nemeth in *The Energy of Money*, [*http://amzn.to/2COcP9R*], talks about trouble at the border. This is a natural phenomenon that happens in expansion. When we are approaching a leap, a new dream, an expansion in consciousness obstacles will come up – the fears, doubts, reasons not to do it. There is a natural tension that arise as we expand. Just know that it is normal and name it as such.

The premise is that when we experience success or greater good in health, wealth, love, relationships or even career, there is a mechanism within us that will operate to return us to "normal."

We are the only ones that can expand our upper limits and lean into a greater awareness of the love, joy, peace, abundance, health and beauty of the Universe. And when we do that, everything changes. As we increase our ability to hold a higher vibration, there will be more to give and more to receive.

Imagine Spirit pouring goodness upon you and you only can receive a portion of it?

There's a parable about going to the ocean and dipping water out of its vastness. The ocean doesn't care whether we use a teaspoon, a coffee cup, a bucket, or a hundred-gallon tanker truck. Its job is simply to be the ocean, and to provide for us all the abundance we could ever want. When we start by believing that the abundance is everywhere, and we can trade our teaspoon for a tanker truck, we engage the possibility that we can raise our capacity to receive.

With the receiving of goodness comes a greater capacity for compassion and love and kindness. Feel into the expansion in your own being as you open to receive.

Often in my work with clients we simply open to receive more awareness of love. How much more love can you receive right now in this moment? Then receive a little bit more.

The surrender process initiates a cycle of clearing, receiving, aligning and clearing again. Each time we expand our capacity to receive, anything unlike it will come up to be healed. When we expand our capacity for love, anything unlike love will come up for a deeper clearing. There is nothing wrong, only some clearing to take place.

When we allow ourselves to come into a greater alignment with Spirit, with the Good that is ours, everything that is out of alignment will come to the surface. Now is the time to clean up some blocks, stop the leaks, and bring a greater coherence to your life. You will know exactly what to do and when. Listen deeply to your heart and soul, it will lead you always to more love and more good.

We get to look, to dive deep once again and see what lurks. There can be resistance in this process. We've done it before and it's time for another house cleaning. What if there was nothing wrong. We clean our houses on a regular basis; we do deep cleaning annually or periodically. It's the same thing.

There are still closets with doors closed; there are still beliefs that are hanging on. Not to worry about it; simply clean them out.

We are in a time of great transformation. We can feel it inside, yet it hasn't appeared on the outer yet. Do not be afraid, do not worry. Begin at a deeper level to trust the process, to believe it is all unfolding as it will. That there really is nothing wrong, we are only on this adventure and journey from the density of human life to the Light that we are.

INTO THE LIGHT PRACTICE

There is a light within us that is yearning to be released. It is getting brighter and brighter and for some reason we appear to be afraid of it. This light is simply part of us, our Essence; our Divinity, our Beingness. Let it out, let it shine. It is not the darkness we are afraid of so much as the fullness of our light. It is there, it is ready and waiting to be accepted. As we are raising our vibrations, we lean into the light for a minute, let it out for a second, or day or week and then quickly retreat. Why are we afraid? Will we trust? Will we be willing to shine?

We are the light of the world, we are the ones we've been waiting for. Let's let our light shine.

PRACTICE

Take a few deep breaths and come into yourself and find the Light within you. You know it well, already. Now it's time to let it have its freedom to light up the room, your life and the world.

Imagine seeing just a little flicker of your own light in a huge dark room. Just a flicker of a small candle flame. It draws your attention. Imagine that as you bring your attention to it, the flame begins to grow. The candle flame now becomes a spotlight. Keep your attention on it with appreciation, wonder, gratitude and amazement. As you do so, the spotlight becomes a lamp post.

Become willing for it to expand even further. Begin an experiment to see how far the light in this lamppost can shine. Expand it to a floodlight. As you do so, imagine you are outside and the floodlight has become the moon, a bright full moon shining on the world. Watch as the moon becomes the very sun. shining in its fullest over the planet.

You are this sun. Imagine that the sun is pouring its light into you and you morph into the sun. you become the light. One with and completely as. From the expansive oneness with this light of sun, feel it focusing down into a pillar of which you are inside.

The pillar is of the brightest light you've ever seen, not fluorescent bright that hurts your eyes, but spirit light that illuminates all things. The pillar decreases in size as it comes to fit the form of your body, but all the while maintaining its brilliance. Feel the very cells of your being vibrating, illuminating with the light that you are. You might feel a tingling or sensation on your skin or in your palms or your chakras. Notice it, allow it.

Imagine yourself going through your days as this radiating being of light. Getting up in the morning, stretching, going through your days, returning to rest in the evening. All as a light being, radiating, pulsating with light.

You are the light of the world. Will you accept it? Will you allow it? Will you become it?

∽

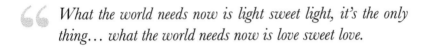 *What the world needs now is light sweet light, it's the only thing… what the world needs now is love sweet love.*

THE WORDS of the classic song are as true today as they have always been. The world is filled with paradox and opposites and in these times as the light is getting stronger, as more and more of us are waking up and being in our light, there appears to be an insurgence of darkness.

It is only coming to the surface to be cleared out. There will always be those who are not of the light, pay them no mind. In keeping our awareness on Light, on Love, in keeping our vibration on light and love, we will begin to see differently. Look more deeply than the nightly news for the good that is happening in humanity. It is there. Find it. Be it. Lead our conversations to the good. Let our thoughts be focused on what we love, the good we see, gratitude, appreciation and yes, forgiveness too. The planet is nearing a tipping point. We are part of the tip into light, into love.

11

SURRENDER

*W*hen I was going through my deep surrender process, it was painful at times, it was some of the hardest work I've ever done, and yet even during it, it was the most rewarding, fulfilling and powerful time. The work when I did it was to acknowledge whatever feeling came up and then dive deep into it – it would take over my body for a time, raging and burning and ultimately purging the deep emotions or beliefs that I'd had for this lifetime and perhaps eternity.

The emotions included anger, fear, rage, guilt, shame, blame, unworthiness, unlovable, not enough-ness We've talked about those already. Then came the surrender of beliefs. All that I held in my belief system came up for release and surrender.

For me, some things were harder to release than others. I was asked to surrender emotions starting with anger and fear. I was also asked to surrender my attachment to material things – my relationships, my stuff, my home, my vocation, my job, my career. Then I was asked to surrender my beliefs – yes, everything I thought to be true had to go; my belief system had to be dismantled to discover a new, truer, more expansive view of the universe.

All this surrender was done inside of a container that I call a spiritual initiation process.

I was being guided by my teacher at the time, but nothing was asked by him, it was Spirit directed. It came from within myself, but beyond myself. I want to make this ultimately clear. There are movements that advocate and even require you to give yourself away to a teacher, a guide, a coach. I do not believe this is good or necessary, in fact it can be quite dangerous.

Surrender is an interesting word, so let's explore it. Surrender is a deep letting go of, a release of the bonds that a given thing/emotion/thought might have on you. It is not being a doormat or a feather flying in the wind, but it is a conscious choice to choose love over and during whatever you are experiencing. If you are angry, can you feel the anger and still choose love? Can you let it burn through you to be fuel for a new fire? If you feel shame, can you feel it all the way through to the other side into love? This is the work of surrender.

Surrender to love is not a platitude or a gloss over or spiritual bypass. The dictionary definition of surrender is to *cease resistance to an enemy or opponent and submit to their authority.* This sounds like war, but it works for our conversation. To surrender is to cease resistance to a thought or belief or emotion that you are experiencing, and to submit to the higher authority of Love and Oneness. When you surrender your (small s), self, you discover who you truly are and who you are becoming.

Love and Oneness cannot coexist with fear or anger in the same plane, and Love and Oneness are always present. Another spiritual paradox. Let's unpack this one.

At any given moment, we are each vibrating at a certain frequency and it can be only one frequency. We have absolute control over the frequency from which we vibrate, as soon as we take that control back from the un- and subconscious. From the physical plane, we can be aligned with a frequency of love or fear, but not at the same time.

There are two planes of existence, one is the physical or relative, the second is the Absolute or Spiritual. The Absolute exists always and forever. It is in a sense a higher plane and can be accessed through conscious awareness, Awakening and any other number of methods. They are co-existing always and from the Absolute we are aware of the relative. From the relative, however, it is easy to be unaware of the Absolute.

The Absolute is where we get Spiritual Truths that resonate, but when used in the relative, they feel like platitudes or spiritual bypass. Beginning to understand that these two planes are different vibrational frequencies, we can use them to surrender.

For example, if I notice that I'm stuck in an emotion with a lower vibrational frequency, I notice that I'm stuck or not feeling well or angry or frustrated, I can catch it and shift it.

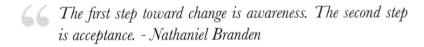 *The first step toward change is awareness. The second step is acceptance. - Nathaniel Branden*

12

BLISS AND THE HARDEST WORK

ystical moments and the journey begins...
Awakening is a beautiful thing. Often our first
Awakening moments offer moments of bliss, the experience of
timelessness, a sense that all is truly well. Time stands still and
a peace that passes all understanding washes over your being.
Your body may become light or even appear to disappear, your
edges become softer. Your mind is either in perfect stillness or
disengaged for the experience. Your heart is wide open,
perhaps even bursting at the seams. There can be a sense that
you've arrived. You've entered the doorway and a new
dimension.

On my first trip to Brazil to spend time with John of God, I
had the most exquisite experience. I had received a spiritual
intervention a couple of days prior and was in an altered state
of consciousness, of bliss, of love. I was doing a ceremony in
the sacred waterfall on the grounds of the Casa. The ritual is
to dunk yourself into the falls twice. The first time is about

release and the second is about receiving. I came to the falls, and placed my feet on the support stones, leaned in so that my head and body were washed over with a stunningly cold, frigid water.

It took my breath away as I felt all that no longer served me wash from my body. Eons of baggage were being washed from the cells of my being. It was a power washing of my inner being. I could feel the water cleansing me and the earth taking it all, welcoming it. I stood back and looked up to the glorious sun, caught my breath and prepared to receive. The second immersion was completely different. I felt the water activating an energy in and through and around me. It was tingly, vibrant and electric. As the water poured over my head and body, the energy permeated and penetrated every cell of my being, As I stepped back this time, I was ignited. The tingling and tremors continued for days, as I integrated the experience.

You know how when you stand up quickly you can get light-headed? This was an experience of being light-bodied.

When this happens bask in it! Bask for as long as possible for it is indeed an Awakening moment. Memorize how it feels in every aspect of your being. Allow as much integration as possible into your experience, into the cells of your being. Let it expand and ground; let it wash you away, leaving you with clear unadulterated bliss. Enjoy it, revel in it, celebrate it. Let it flow, but don't try too hard to hold on to it.

Then the work of the journey begins. For some, the experience changes everything at depth, but for most of us, it is the beginning, the starting point, the kick off to a journey that could continue for all time. This is often surprising. From the expanded place of bliss and Oneness, why would there be any work to do at all?

I realized, many years after my own Awakening began, that our spiritual journey is a journey of descent into humanity, moving into the illusion of separation to experience all that it means to be human. At first it appears to be an opening and expansive experience, then very quickly it becomes the work of a lifetime.

Humanity, as I'm using it here is the fullness of our experience on planet earth; the good and bad, beautiful and ugly. It is the fullness of experiencing our life and the emotions that come with it. It is things going well and not so well; it is exhilaration and grief. It is success and failure, happiness and sadness; being in the flow and out of the flow. As we embrace our humanity, we begin again to come into awareness of Spirit. Our Light, our Spirit vibrates at a high frequency, becoming human lowers that vibration into the density of this planet and our Awakening raises the frequency once again.

It is in this time that many are Awakening to the Oneness, some are beginning to understand. It is a concept beyond the current recognition of the masses, but it is happening all around us every day. The current understanding is pointing in the direction of the great Truth, the Truth that will change the planet. The Truth that we are One, that Love is the foundation of the universe. It's time for all of us to dive deep and come into realization of this deeper Truth. It is happening, it will happen, and the time is now.

The Awakening journey is an evolutionary journey in consciousness. It is the process of moving in consciousness from a limited and dense human experience of separation, which is the planetary norm, into a new dimension of consciousness, one of Oneness, a return to original goodness, a higher vibration and a return to Love. The doorways are opening, and we are catching moments. But to live there, to remain in an expanded heart space of love and connection we must clear the old, dismantle and surrender all that is unlike love.

For some, a traumatic experience can cause Awakening and a release of all unlike love, but for most of us, it is more of a systematic process of unraveling the old and weaving the new into our current lives. Anita Moorjani talks about her near-death experience and how it caused her Awakening where everything changed, in her book, *Dying to be Me*, [*http://amzn.to/2CjwvFu*] For her the experience of uncondi-tional love washed over her in ways that healed her terminal illness, changed her consciousness and ultimately redirected her entire life.

The moments of mystical experience, the moments of pure bliss are touchstones, doorways we are being introduced to.

With each touch of bliss, the journey begins again. Watch for anything and everything that is unlike love, for it is appearing to be surrendered and transcended. Pay attention to what shows up in your life over the next few weeks. Do you get surprisingly angry or fearful? Do your old thoughts of unwor-thiness or discounting your experience show up? Do you feel unsettled in your body or life? If so, these are all indicators of the next layers to be processed through.

My first glimpse into the power of this truth was many years after I'd been teaching it. I thought I knew love, I thought I was love, I thought I was aligned and embodied as Love and to a degree that was true. Then I had a mystical experience in which my heart broke wide open and I fell − like Alice in Wonderland as she fell down the rabbit's hole − I slipped through a portal of sorts and landed right in the center of myself and the Universe. On my way through the portal, I experienced my life, I saw with new eyes; the black and white television turned high definition, vibrant color. And that doesn't even begin to describe the experience, because it was visceral not visual. It was complete and total.

It was as if the very DNA of my being was being restrung - it was as if I entered the very television screen I was watching. Remember the movie Pleasantville? When the two teenagers fell into a television show that was black and white? The characters brought innovative ideas to the town, ultimately the others began to see in color, things changed. It was the sort of that. It was falling into a greater dimension, into a greater awareness.

The colors were fresher and more vibrant, the air even felt different entering my lungs. It was clear and clean. I, for a moment, had let go of all judgment, surrendered anything that was unlike Love.

I had entered bliss. I was One with all that is. I thought I had arrived once and for all. Life was brilliant and beautiful. I was expanded and love. I remained in this altered state for a couple of weeks. My teacher simply smiled and said, now the work will begin again. And it did. This moment was the start of another layer of a spiritual surrender.

My experience is the greater the bliss, the deeper the surrender that will follow it. The work, as we've touched on is exquisite and excruciating. The work is the hardest work you'll ever do, and so well worth it. The stripping, the unclenching, the burning, the ripping out of old, and no longer necessary beliefs and patterns is deep and profound.

We must go at the speed of our soul; going too fast, or giving your authority to an outside influence can result in a more difficult journey, it may even damage the psyche. So, please, if you are on a journey of Awakening, of surrender, be sure you are supported by someone who is guiding you to your higher wisdom. The journey has begun, you are on it, so surrender deeply into the process and go at your own pace. There is not necessarily a reward for getting there quicker. The journey is as important as the destination.

13

ONENESS IN TWO WORLDS

On this planet, we live and move and have our experience. In Spirit we are One humanity, One planet, One race that is Human. To be human is an evolutionary process. Just as most of our children, when born go through a learning process that has a typical progression. First, we learn to sit, then stand, to crawl and walk. Then we learn to talk. There is the school system from pre-school, through high school. For some, the learning process continues to advanced-learning, and perhaps additional degrees.

As a humanity we are ever evolving as well. Many of us are reaching the advanced degrees of Awakening, of love, compassion and kindness. Others however, are still in consciousness kindergarten, which means they are either still asleep or beginning to wake up. This is not about judgement; rather, it is about compassion. If you are reading this, you are in advance degrees. You likely have had many lifetimes of spiritual awareness.

Many of our way-showers, spiritual teachers, mystics and shamans speak of walking in two worlds. A common phrase is "be in the world, but not of it." We are spiritual beings having a human experience. We are living in this world, but we do not have to be bound by it. There is much more to creation that the world we live in. There is so much beyond this world that can impact and shift our awareness, yet we are called to be in the world even as we awaken to a bigger truth.

It is critical now to bring our spirituality off the mountain tops and privacy of our inner world to the outer world. To be engaged with the world we live in and the earth we walk upon. To get our heads out of the clouds and our feet moving on the earth.

Spirituality has historically stayed out of social activism and politics. So many of the social activist issues are now convoluted into political issues. Even in the midst, we are being called to be a stand for humanity, for kindness, for equality, for love. We are called to stand out against war and violence, discrimination and hate, however, the stand against is not nearly as powerful as the stand for. Become aware of where you place your stakes, are you against something or for something else? Which feels more spiritually powerful? To stand for is expansive and powerful. To stand against tends to lean into what we don't want rather than what we do want. It is a subtle yet profound difference.

There is a movement now of spiritual activism, of enlightened social activism, not as a political movement, but as our responsibility as awakened people to join together for the greater good of humanity. AGNT.Today (Association for Global New Thought) is inviting us to stand #BoldlyTogether. From their website [*https://www.agnt.today/*]: Engaged spirituality that inspires the individual life and empowers social uplift is the mission of the Association for Global New Thought. "We stand with a Conscious Majority of the worlds' people who know that by connecting, supporting, and mobilizing one another toward the Common Good, we can create a world that works through everyone. Something has been stirring in the collective unconscious of humanity, now finding its way to the surface of society though conscious, awakened beings everywhere."

We live in and on this planet, yet we are not of it. We are greater than this world, in consciousness and being. This planet, our beautiful little blue marble of existence is a learning field, a school for humanity or a drama production. Life will give us what we need for growth, what we signed up for prior to coming and it gives us incredible opportunities for fast pace, quick-action spiritual growth.

Look and see what you see, feel what you feel and choose love. That is the fast track and the only tried and true method to achieve and become Oneness.

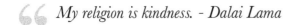 *My religion is kindness. - Dalai Lama*

The outer expression of Oneness is kindness and compassion. To be kind is to express Oneness. Being kind does no harm, being kind can touch a heart and heal a soul. Being kind is a simple habit that will change the world. Let's begin right here and right now to be kind. While we want to be kind globally, let's start at home.

Be kind to yourself. Be kind to You! Your body, your emotions, your past, your present, your heart and soul. That means love yourself. Quit throwing insults your way, stop the noise in your mind about being less than or unworthy. Do whatever it takes to rewrite the scripts you play in your head, especially the unconscious ones.

Begin to love yourself with unadulterated kindness. Look yourself in the eyes and tell yourself kind things. Begin to be kind and love will show up. Begin to love yourself and kindness will show up. Watch those thoughts, the things you tell yourself. This can change your life if you practice.

14

CAPACITY TO RECEIVE

*T*hrough our life experiences we become hard wired at certain set points. We touched on this with our discussion on upper limits. We experience and allow and expect a certain level of health, wealth, love, and blessings and beyond that we either don't see them, don't allow them or push it away.

The set point keeps us stable. For example, if we are generally healthy and something happens to our health, we are more apt to bounce back, to recover and to return to set point. If you carry a tendency to unhealthy, that is where you will return again and again, even after doing much to create greater health, until you change your set point.

The same principle is true with love, time and even money, we each have an invisible, unconscious set point. It is and was created by our experiences, our beliefs, the things that we were told as a child. If your set point is to be receiving $50,000 each year as an annual salary and you suddenly get a new position that pays double; unless you reset your previous set point, you will experience discomfort; you might have a major repair or unexpected expense. Some people also experience other challenges with a quick expansion, a health or relationship issue.

We see this repeatedly with people who win the lottery. They have an average lifestyle, win the big one and within a couple of years are typically worse off financially than before.

The same is true for our capacity to receive Love or to hold an awakened vibration. After a moment of bliss or a mystical experience, one typically holds a new vibration and way of being for a short while. Then over time perhaps a few weeks or months, there is a tendency to return to the original set point.

Please understand that I'm not talking about material things, so much as Spiritual ones. Ask yourself what is my ability to receive right now? From 1 – 100? Where is it? Can you build your receiving muscle, stretching it by 10% or more?

Our practice and the work becomes ever-increasing our capacity to receive. In Awakening, can you receive more love and light? Can you receive a greater perspective? Can you receive the guidance that will turn your life around and make a bigger impact in the world? Can you trade your teaspoon in for a bucket?

For some there can be a feeling of "let down" or depression even after an expansion in awareness or consciousness. It can come as a surprise and can take your breath away with the contrast. This is a normal experience, called the Expansion Hangover. There are ways to navigate through it with ease and not return to the former set point.

When we expand quickly without a solid support system, everything in the boat is rocked; the balance is unsettled, and things tend to crash. We see this as evidence in a state of mind that wondered when the other shoe will fall. It's too good to be true. Something will bring me back. These are belief systems that can be shifted, changed and adjusted. It doesn't not have to be that way.

The first step is to become conscious of what is holding you. Where is your set point? Imagine it being like a thermostat in your heating and air conditioning system.

If you have an automated system that controls both heat and cooling, set at 75 degrees, when the house gets hotter than that, the air kicks in. If it gets cooler, the heat kicks in. Everything in that system is working to keep the set point at 75 degrees.

Become aware of where your set points are. Where can you easily raise them to allow more good into your life? Where can you increase your capacity to receive kindness? Abundance? Love? Health? Time? Productivity? Fun? Leisure? Spiritual awareness?

As I've become aware of my own set points, it becomes easier to feel them before they hit, hard and I can consciously lean in to expand but that wasn't always the case. A couple of years ago I was on a trip of a lifetime and hit a set point that stopped me. Literally. We were in Bali, on a 15-day spiritual pilgrimage with a group of 60 of our new best friends. I was immersing myself in the spiritual expansion; being completely transformed by the sites we were visiting and the sacred rituals we were participating in. I was totally in my element and enjoying the experience, when not half way through the trip, I tripped and fell off a curb. I went down, down, down all the way into the street and knew immediately it was not a good thing.

Here's an interesting observation. A group of six of us had gone to dinner. Two of them were fast walkers, and were way ahead of us, trying to catch our ride back to our resort. My husband and another couple were lagging far behind, deep in a conversation. I found myself, alone, lying in the street in a foreign country with no one to help me. I had lost my friends and my support. You could assume that I was ungrounded or expanding too fast. You could even make the leap to some other story about not feeling supported, as ankles represent not only outer support, but also the inner support structures. It was only a matter of moments before I stood up and my husband was there to support me.

I realized quickly that it was an upper limit problem, that my set point was about to be rewired in an expanded way and I was in trouble at the border. In my spiritual expansion, I was rewiring an inner support structure that would take time to integrate. Turns out I tore a ligament in my ankle that kept me grounded and had my attention for almost a year. Even to this day, I am aware of my ankle and the places that I'm craving support and I'm able to provide that for myself or ask for it from others. What is my capacity to receive support and how am I asking for support are two questions that keep me increasing my set points?

A set point can be seen as the boundary awareness. It is the box in which we live, even if we are limitless and box-less. The edges of our consciousness are fluid and ever expanding. The set point problems only arise when we become rigid. An effortless way to flow with increasing our capacity to receive is to stay fluid, to be ever expanding your awareness, your capacity to see and be beauty in the world.

Here's a totally different example of set points. My husband

and I live on a beautiful lake, we have kayaks and we have a great beach just around the corner, a 2-minute drive from the house. When we moved here we made a conscious choice to have more fun; to spend more time on the water either on the kayak or at the beach. This is our second summer here and already our capacity to be in and on the water, has apparently diminished.

We still go onto the water and every time we do we say; "we should do this more." One day, I suggested that we take the afternoon off and kayak. My husband, Rob, was heading out to get busy, but he caught himself and said, "Yes, I can go later to do this project". We so enjoyed the time, we let it be lazy and relaxed.

Here's what we noticed. We each have a tendency and a belief system that causes us to work hard, to not take the time for play and relaxation that we desire. His message from child-hood says he should be productive, or working on a project to be ok, holding a belief of "it's much better to work than to play." I was holding a pattern of "there's too much to do, I must keep plugging away to get it all done. It's better to be busy than to relax and play."

The truth, the greater truth, is we both could increase our capacity to receive more relaxation, more enjoyment of doing nothing at all. This is the experience we have when we take time to be in or on the water.

How much Awakening can you receive? How can you lean in and be open to more; more clarity, connection, spiritual aware-ness? How much love can you receive? What is your capacity to receive not only love but also goodness? Where do you stop receiving? If you are new to receiving, it might be quite low. Can you accept a compliment? Will you allow someone to buy you dinner or coffee or a gift? Can you let others help you? These are all indicators of a set point. The general capacity to receive is related to your capacity to awaken.

How do you respond to an unexpected gift? With awe and appreciation, gratitude and receptivity? Or do you begin to shut down? Do you say, I couldn't possibly?

Where can you easily and gently increase your capacity to receive? Where can you easily and gently increase your capacity for improved health, increased abundance, more fun and play? Where can you profoundly increase your capacity for love? To be love, to see love, to radiate love, to give love?

The work is to open the pathways consciously. To see the abundance and glory and possibility all around you and then to take advantage of it; to use the beauty to increase your connection to that which is greater than you.

As we are Awakening and raising our vibrations, our capacity to receive expands until it doesn't. When you notice a set point, or a stopping point, it is time to expand, to rise, to allow even more good into your consciousness, into your system and into your life. For you are the one we are waiting for. We all are.

RECEIVE LOVE PRACTICE

Take a few deep breaths and come into yourself. Become aware of your heart. Feel your feet touching the floor and allow them to anchor to the earth. Lift your awareness from the crown of your head and your palms and imagine being connected to the Sun and through the sun to the universe.

Let the connections between the earth and the sun expand you, feel that you are part of something so much greater than your current experience of being in human form. Feel yourself being stretched ever so gently and expanded in awareness.

Place your hand on your heart and feel it beating. This heart is both the organ in your body that keeps you living, and your connection to your spiritual heart. Imagine your heart opening to love, to feeling love, to receiving love. Focus on love (or gratitude or appreciation) in your heart space for a few breaths.

Notice that your body shifts and changes, you become more relaxed. Let the love, gratitude, appreciation overflow your heart and fill your torso. Do not force it, simply allow it or imagine it. Begin to receive from above a flow (thread, trickle, gush) of love from the Universe into you. It's gentle, it's warm, it's beautiful. Let it fill your heart space, which is now greater than your physical heart. Let it fill this space so that it begins to expand. Your heart space filled with love, is filling your torso, it is expanding so far that it extends from your body forward and back, from side to side.

Keep breathing and allowing; receiving. Feel, allow, imagine that your heart space expands so far that you find yourself standing right in the middle of it. Like a huge bubble of purity. Take a few moments to feel this love that you are now standing in the midst of, permeate, penetrate and fill the interspaces of your being. Let it wash away hurts or rough edges, softening the places that are hard, let it fill you like water on a parched desert. How much more can you receive? How much more can you expand?

Take a few moments to anchor in the experience. How does it feel, what do you notice? Sounds? Taste? Smell? Seeing? Touching? Put a word or a phrase on your experience and know that you can return here again and again. The infinite has unlimited love, abundance, health, time, joy, peace and more for you now and always.

Take a few deep breaths and placing your hand on your heart, give thanks.

When you are ready, open your eyes. And so it is.

15

WHAT'S COMING

*a*ll is well. What if you knew in your bones and in your thoughts that all is well? What if this statement was not only a platitude, but a frequency that resonates as true? What if you knew without a doubt that you did not have to hold back anything, that whoever you are and whatever you do is exactly perfect for you? What if you knew you never had to dumb down another conversation, that people either meet you or not, with where you are and what you want to share.

Let it go. Let it go. Let it go a million times until it doesn't want to come back any longer. What am I letting go? What are you letting go? What others think about you. What you think others think about what you are thinking.

In fact, the truth is no one is thinking about you. No one cares about you. That sounds callous, but back away from taking it personally a bit and realize the truth. It's not that no one cares about You, but that no one cares about your incessant worrying about what they are thinking about what you are thinking or doing.

When you are worried about what others are thinking about you, look again and see what they are thinking. Most them are either thinking about what you might be thinking or not thinking about you at all.

We are in a culture that is so self-absorbed that no one pays any attention. And we are the Ones, we've been waiting for. We are the ones that are raising the bars, that are the way showers for others. Be not concerned about what others think about you and be completely aware that all you are impacts those around you. Yes, one final paradox to consider.

You are a beloved creation of Spirit. You are a uniquely you flower of beauty with all your thorns and sticklers and everything. Embrace the spiritual paradox and lean into the becoming of who you already are.

And so, it continues, our journey of Awakening and life on this planet. We are the same and yet totally different. Totally different and yet the same. The Awakening process does not mean that life quits happening. We do not have the luxury of going up on a mountain top and living our days out in peace. We are called to be on the planet, to ground the energies of Awakening into normal everyday life. We are here to be the Light workers, the way-showers and we are leading (creating/making/purging) forging the way into a new consciousness.

After the first moments of bliss in Awakening, it becomes the hardest work you'll ever do, and it does not have to be hard. We are felling trees (beliefs and patterns) that have stood centuries. But if we know there are trees to fell both in the world and first in our own being and consciousness, there is no suffering in it. One of my favorite authors, Paul Selig says it best in his book, *I am The Word;[http://amzn.to/2Crvw57]*:

> *If you don't know that trees have to fall then every time one does, you are traumatized, but if you know that trees fall then when you come across another one down, you can simply step over it with no attachment or drama around it. - Paul Selig*

The trees down are our former belief systems; it is our habitual patterns of thinking and being. The trees down will become the structures for living as a separated human. With each structure down, another and new one is created; one that is much freer, light, lifted and expansive. With this awareness, celebrate the ones that fall.

We are divine beings, we have a light within us that is beyond anything we can yet imagine, even as we have experienced it more than a few times. Our work is to continue integrating the light with our Spirit. To continue opening, receiving and containing the energies, the higher vibrations that are wanting to come through us.

We are One, you and I and the support from the invisible realms. The connection we seek is not outside of us, it is within. We are the collective.

Years ago, I came into a relationship with my guides and angels. For decades I've felt them with me and would lean onto them when I remembered to. I would ask questions and seek guidance from that which was still connected to me, but was outside of me. Then I had the experience upon asking where my guides were, and I could not find access to them. I discovered in a moment of clarity that I am One with them in another new and subtle yet profound way. That which was outside of me is now within me. My vibration has come into a new alignment and once again, I begin again.

This is a message that I received from the depth of my soul on that day:

We are One, Spirit is not separate from us. *No longer will we be asked to search outside of ourselves. No longer is there a need for outer confirmation or clarification. All that Spirit is, you are. All that Spirit is, you have access to. The veil is getting very thin and it is up to you to dissolve it completely. Lean into this truth. Lean into this expansion, for this is the moment in this lifetime you have been awaiting.* We are being asked to fully integrate this Oneness, to access the Infinite Spirit from within.

The time is now, you are ready. We have in the past, looked around like the fish in the ocean wondering where the water is. But breathe in and Spirit is here; breathe out and Spirit is present here. Waking, sleeping, walking, working, resting, playing, Spirit is here. When you expand and lean into Spirit you find it within. When you are contracted and having a harder time connecting, Spirit is present. Pierce the limit you are bumping up again and be aware once more that you are filled with Spirit.

Spirit says, "We are with you always, in and through and as you. We are a collective that has no separation; and you are part of it. It is the collective of Light and love on the planet."

It is the collective of Awakening, of the growing edge of consciousness as humanity comes closer to the quantum leap of evolution into Oneness. It is real. Quantum physics, spiral dynamics and David Hawkins work in consciousness; Access consciousness; or other modalities, they are all indicating an event like never before on our planet. The Awakening is happening. The clearing is happening. Never mind what it looks like in the outer world right now; there is a polarity happening, a separation of those willing and able to shift from those still mired in fear and hatred, competition and comparison; judgement and resistance.

Love is the answer, love is the way. Light is the power, and the path. You are love and light embodied. Let your light so shine. Come into your greatness; come into your power. Lean into the energy that you are, yes, even as it is too much for your system. You are being stretched, prepared, and expanded. Lean into it, do not be afraid. It is this for which you are on the planet. It's time and you are ready.

For Aliza's paperback books, you may visit her her:
http://www.divine-Awakening.org/alizas-links/

Touching hearts, freeing souls and transforming lives. Aliza Bloom Robinson, vibrational catalyst, speaker, author and minister is committed to the Awakening of our world, which will result in the end of suffering and the rise of Love, purpose, passion and connection.

Aliza is the author of *Falling Into Ease – Release Your Struggle and Create a Life You Love*; the companion, *Falling Into Ease Guidebook – Simple Everyday Practices to Release Struggle and Create Ease*; *Be a BOA, (Bold, Outrageous, Authentic) Not A Constrictor* eBook; and *What is Mine to Do – A Guided Process for Spiritual Discernment* eBook. [*http://amzn.to/2CAV2pB*]

She is a contributing author in the Best Selling 365 Series: *365 Ways to Connect with Your Soul; 365 Moments of Grace; 365 Life Shifts;* and *A Coaches Collaborative.*

She enjoys life with her husband, living in both Arizona and Arkansas and spending time with their 15 grandchildren.

FOR YOUR KINDLE, IPAD, OR READING ON THE GO — ALIZA'S EBOOKS ARE HERE:

1. *Falling Into Ease – Release Your Struggle and Create A Life You Love http://amzn.to/2CmjrLC*
2. *Falling Into Ease Guidebook – Simple Everyday Practices to Release Struggle and Create Ease http://amzn.to/2lPKDev*
3. *Be A B.O.A., Not A Constrictor eBook http://amzn.to/2EQHaoK*
4. *What Is Mine To Do…? A Guided Process for Spiritual Discernment eBook http://amzn.to/2CAV2pB*

WHERE TO FIND ALIZA ON THE WEB

1. Center for Divine Awakening – *http://www.divine-Awakening.org/center-for-divine-Awakening/*
2. Aliza Bloom — *http://AlizaBloom.com*
3. Aliza's News & Announcements on Facebook — *https://www.facebook.com/divineAwakeningaliza/*
4. Aliza's Private Facebook Group – *http://www.facebook.com/groups/findingease/*
5. YouTube – *http://bit.ly/AlizaYouTube*
6. Twitter – *http://twitter.com/AlizaBloom*
7. Instagram – *https://wwwlinstagram.com/aliza.robinson/*
8. LinkedIn – *http://bit.ly/LinkedAliza*

ADDITIONAL RESOURCES FOR YOUR JOURNEY

1. You Can't Sleep Through Your Awakening by Rev. Dr. Jane Simmons - *http://amzn.to/2EOJcFT*
2. I am The Word by Paul Selig - *http://amzn.to/2Crvw57*
3. Conscious Evolution by Barbara Marx Hubbard, Website - *https://www.barbaramarxhubbard.com/*
4. Conscious Evolution - *http://amzn.to/2Cjv3ik*
5. Spiral Dynamics by Don Beck, Website - *http://www.spiraldynamics.net/*
6. Spiral Dynamics: Mastering Values, Leadership and Change - *http://amzn.to/2CminHC*
7. The Big Leap by Gay Hendricks - *http://amzn.to/2CxoFIi*
8. Energy of Money by Dr. Maria Nemeth - *http://amzn.to/2COcP9R*
9. The Likely Cause of Addiction Has Been Discovered, and It Is Not What You Think - Article in Huffington Post by Johann Hari - *http://bit.ly/addictionHari*
10. Dying to be Me by Anita Moorjani - *http://amzn.to/2CjwvFu*
11. AGNT.Today (Association for Global New Thought) - *https://www.agnt.today*

CPSIA information can be obtained
at www.ICGtesting.com
Printed in the USA
FFHW020653210119
50171658-55121FF